Collins English Li

Series editors: K R Cripwell and Lewis

A library of graded readers for students
language, and for reluctant native read
levels of difficulty. Structure, vocabular
all controlled according to principles lai... in detail in *A Guide to Collins English Library*. A list of the books follows. Numbers after each title indicate the level at which the book is written: 1 has a basic vocabulary of 300 words and appropriate structures, 2 : 600 words, 3 : 1000 words, 4 : 1500 words, 5 : 2000 words and 6 : 2500 words.

Inspector Holt and the Fur Van John Tully 1
Where is Bill Ojo? John Tully 1
Crocodile! K R Cripwell 1
Four Short Stories Margery Morris 1
The Story of Macbeth from Shakespeare 1
Fast Money K R Cripwell 1
It's a Trick! Lewis Jones 1
Taxi! Jane Homeshaw 1
Tin Lizzie Jane Homeshaw 1
Dead in the Morning Jane Homeshaw 1
Letters from the Dead Jane Homeshaw 1
The Pathfinders Jane Homeshaw 1
Cats in the Dark John Tully 1
Journey to Universe City Leslie Dunking 1
Three Folk Tales Margaret Naudi 1
Inspector Holt and the Chinese Necklace John Tully 1
Fastline UK Jane Homeshaw 1
The Man with Three Fingers John Tully 1
Inspector Holt Gets His Man John Tully 2
The Bridge John Tully 2
Muhammad Ali: King of the Ring John Tully 2
The Magic Garden K R Cripwell 2
The Wrestler K R Cripwell 2
The Titanic is Sinking K R Cripwell 2
The Canterville Ghost Oscar Wilde 2
The Prince and the Poor Boy Mark Twain 2
Two Roman Stories from Shakespeare 2
Oliver Twist Charles Dickens 2
The Story of Madame Tussaud's Lewis Jones 2
Three Sherlock Holmes Adventures Sir A Conan Doyle 2
The Story of Scotland Yard Lewis Jones 2
Charles and Diana Margery Morris 2
The Charlie Chaplin Story Jane Homeshaw 2
A King's Love Story K R Cripwell 2
Dangerous Earth Jane Homeshaw 2
Chariots of Fire W J Weatherby 2
Shark Attack! Jane Keane 2
The Complete Robot: Selected Stories Isaac Asimov 2
Roadie Chris Banks 2
The Mystery of Dr Fu Manchu Sax Rohmer 2

Five Ghost Stories Viola Huggins 3
Brainbox and Bull Michael Kenyon 3
Climb a Lonely Hill Lilith Norman 3
Custer's Gold Kenneth Ulyatt 3
The Gunshot Grand Prix Douglas Rutherford 3
Born Free Joy Adamson 3
Cinema Stunts K R Cripwell 3
David Copperfield Charles Dickens 3
Three English Kings from Shakespeare 3
An American Tragedy Theodore Dreiser 3
Six American Stories Norman Wymer 3
Emma and I Sheila Hocken 3
Maimunah David Hill 3
Little Women Louisa M Alcott 3
Marilyn Monroe Peter Dainty 3
Bruce Springsteen Toni Murphy 3
The Picture of Dorian Gray Oscar Wilde 3
Is That It? Bob Geldof 3
The White South Hammond Innes 4
Landslide Desmond Bagley 4
Nothing is the Number when you Die Joan Fleming 4
The Lovely Lady and Other Stories D H Lawrence 4
King Solomon's Mines H Rider Haggard 4
A Christmas Carol Charles Dickens 4
Jane Eyre Charlotte Bronte 4
Pride and Prejudice Jane Austen 4
Dr Jekyll and Mr Hyde R L Stevenson 4
Huckleberry Finn Mark Twain 4
The African Child Camara Laye 4
Airport International Brian Moynahan 4
The Secret Sharer and Other Sea Stories Joseph Conrad 4
Death in Vienna? K E Rowlands 4
Hostage Tower Alistair MacLean/John Denis 4
The Potter's Wheel Chukwuemeka Ike 4
Campbell's Kingdom Hammond Innes 4
The Guns of Navarone Alistair MacLean 5
Where Eagles Dare Alistair MacLean 5
I Know my Love Catherine Gaskin 5
The Wreck of the Mary Deare Hammond Innes 5
The Eagle has Landed Jack Higgins 5
The Mayor of Casterbridge Thomas Hardy 5
Wuthering Heights Emily Bronte 5
Sense and Sensibility Jane Austen 5
Middlemarch George Eliot 5
Victory Joseph Conrad 5
Experiences of Terror Roland John 5
Japan: Islands in the Mist Peter Milward 5
The Glory Boys Gerald Seymour 6
Harry's Game Gerald Seymour 6
Hard Times Charles Dickens 6
Doctor Zhivago Boris Pasternak 6
Sons and Lovers D H Lawrence 6
Vanity Fair William Thackeray 6

Collins English Library Level 1

TIN LIZZIE

THE STORY OF HENRY FORD

JANE HOMESHAW

Illustrations by Campbell Kennedy

Collins: London and Glasgow

Fourth edition 1987

Printed and published in Great Britain by
William Collins Sons and Co Ltd
Glasgow G4 0NB

First published in Collins English Library, 1980

We are grateful to The Ford Motor Co. Ltd. for permission to reproduce the photograph used on the cover and those on pp 17, 22, 25 and 29.
We are also grateful to the Mansell Collection Ltd. for permission to reproduce the photograph on p 26.

ISBN 0 00 370143 3

The Tin Box

"The fire's good and hot now!"

"Yes," said a small boy. "You can begin!"

Two of the boys placed a tin box on top of the fire. Two more put water into it.

"More trees for the fire!" said the small boy. " . . . And get more water!"

A girl came out of Miller School. "What *are* you doing?" she asked. It was Margaret, the small boy's sister.

"The fire's making hot water," he said. "Then the hot steam from the water can drive the wheels round."

"What wheels?" she asked.

"Those wheels on the tin box. Can't you see them?"

Margaret's eyes went to the box.

"Oh yes! I can see them now!"

"It's my new engine," said the boy. "Look! The wheels are going round now!"

"They're going very fast!" said Margaret. "Is it OK?"

"Engines *are* fast . . . " said the boy. Then he stopped. Because it wasn't OK. Something was very wrong! In front of his eyes, the tin box went up three metres into the air! Hot water landed on

some of the boys. A finger of fire touched one of the school buildings.

"Fire! Fire!"

"There's a fire at the school!"

"Water! Get some water!"

The small boy with the thin face walked across to the tin box, now on the ground, and eyed the wheels. They still went round.

Round and round.

Miller School was in Dearborn, Michigan, US. The year was 1873. The name of the small boy was Henry Ford. He was ten years old.

The Steam-Engine

"Henry! Get up! It's eight o'clock!" said Margaret. "There's a lot of work this morning!"

"Go away!" answered Henry. "Work! There's always work in this place!"

"Father's going into Detroit this morning!" said Margaret.

"Oh!" said Henry, and jumped out of bed.

It was a July morning in 1876. Henry Ford was thirteen. He lived with his father and brothers and

"The tin box went up three metres into the air!"

sister on land near the village of Dearborn. William Ford, his father, was a farmer. He loved his land and farmed it well. William was up at six every morning. He worked from morning to night. Then he went to bed. That was his life.

"Where were *you* this morning, Henry?" The family were at the breakfast table. The speaker was John, one of Henry's brothers.

"What time this morning?"

"Six o'clock."

"At six o'clock, I was asleep in bed," said Henry. "I was asleep at seven o'clock too. Why? Where were you?"

"I was down by the trees with Father. We've got some more wood from the trees. Father's going to sell the wood in Detroit today. Men must work or they don't get any money for food!"

"Some people can work with their heads, not with their backs," said Henry. "Horses work with their backs. But I'm not an animal! I'm a man!"

"You're not a man! You're a boy!" said John.

"One day I'm going to be a man. And I'm not going to work on a farm then!" said Henry.

"What are you going to do?" William, Henry's father, asked.

"I'm going to build engines. Engines for farm-work. One day, there aren't going to be any more horses on farms. But there are going to be a lot of engines!"

John looked up in the air and touched his head

with one finger. "My poor brother!" he said to the family round the table. "He's a little wrong in the head! We must be very good to him! Perhaps he's ill!" He put his hand on Henry's head. "Yes . . . Your head's very hot! Go back to bed! Poor boy! Poor boy!"

"You're asking for a fight!" said Henry. He looked at his father. "Dad. Can I come to Detroit with you this morning?"

"OK," said William. "Go and get the horses ready."

It was a long, fifteen kilometre drive into Detroit. The horses were slow and the weather was very hot. But William was happy behind his horses. He loved them like children.

"Beautiful animals!" he said to his son. "Without horses, men can never work the land!"

"Why can't you do the work with steam-engines?" Henry asked.

"Steam-engines are no good on the land," said William. "They're OK for trains. But you can't drive them on roads or on fields."

"Why not?" asked Henry.

"Steam-engines want a big fire and a lot of water. So they must be big. You can't drive them on fields or on country roads . . . "

The horses walked on through the hot morning. Henry was near to sleep. Then, through half shut

eyes, he saw a tall grey line of steam. It went from the ground, up into the sky.

"What's that?" said William. "There are no trains here!"

Henry looked again. Under the line of steam, there was a big tin box on wheels! And, on top of the tin box, there was a man!

"It's a steam-engine!" Henry jumped down and went up to the driver. "Hello," he said. "Is this *your* steam-engine?"

"No," said the man. "I only work with it."

"What work do you do?"

"Oh! We work on farms!" said the driver. "We get trees out of the ground . . . get wood from trees . . ."

Henry looked at his father. "You were wrong, Dad!" he said.

William Ford walked up to the man. "I'm William Ford," he said. "And this is my son, Henry."

"My name's Fred Reden," said the driver. "So . . . Henry likes engines . . . Perhaps he can come and work with me sometimes. Then he can learn more about them."

"Oh Dad! Can I go with Mr Reden?"

"OK," said William. "But not today."

That night, on the way home, Henry said to his father, "You were wrong, Dad! Engines *can* work in fields!"

"Perhaps," answered Mr Ford. "But that steam-engine today was very slow. How fast can it

"Under the line of steam, there was a big tin box on wheels!"

go? Eight kilometres an hour? My horses can run fifteen kilometres in an hour!"

"Yes. You're right," said Henry. "But one day, I'm going to build a fast engine. One day I'm going to drive from Detroit to Dearborn in half an hour!"

"One day! One day!" said William Ford.

The Question . . . and the Answer

All the world wanted it. Young men in every country looked for it. In 1885, it was the big question of the day.

They had trains, and now they had bicycles. But they wanted something more . . .

They wanted a car.

A car can stand in front of your house. You can walk out of your door and get into it. You can drive fast to any place. Then you can get out and your car stops there. After a little time, you get into your car again and go back home. Or you can go to the shops, the bank, into town or out to the country. And you can get to all these places *fast*.

In 1885, the big question was – 'What is going to drive the wheels round?' Steam-engines were no good. The world wanted a small, fast engine.

Men in many countries looked for the answer. In Germany, there were Benz and Daimler and

Otto. In France, there were Panhard and Bouton. In America, there were Olds and Maxim and the Duryea Brothers.

In America, the answer came to Maxim. Gasoline!

Maxim put a very little gasoline into a long tin box. Then, he put a match into the box and jumped back fast. He jumped because the air around him was alive with fire! Maxim had his answer. From only a little gasoline and a lot of air, you can get a very big fire! The hot air can drive the wheels round. And so, Maxim had his gasoline engine.

After a time people learned about Maxim's gasoline engine. They all wanted to make one too.

The Bad Days

In 1891 Henry Ford was twenty-eight. He had a wife, Clara. He had a house and some land. Like his father, Henry was a farmer. He still liked engines. He often went to the engine-shops in Detroit and talked to the engineers there. But he still worked on the land. Still only a farmer.

Then, one day, he came home from town very happy. "We're going to live in Detroit!" he said to his wife, Clara. Clara wasn't happy about that. She liked Dearborn. All her family and friends were there. But she was a good wife so she said nothing.

"I've got work with the Edison Company," he said. "I'm going to be their night-engineer. I'm going to get $45 a month!"

"That's a lot of money," said Clara. "We don't make $45 here on the land."

"There's something more," said Henry. And he talked to her about the new gasoline engines.

"*I* can make engines like that too," he said. "I can sell them for a lot of money."

"How can you do that?" asked Clara.

"Get me a pencil," said Henry. On the back of a page from an old book, he pencilled a picture.

"There you are!" he said. "That's my engine! What do you think about it?"

"It's very good!" said Clara. (She was a very good wife!) "So. When do we go?"

It was only November. But the weather in November 1893 was very bad. After his night's work at the Edison Company, Henry always walked home. It was a long, cold walk.

In 1893 Henry Ford was very poor. He still got $45 a month. And a house and food cost a lot of money in Detroit. And that wasn't all. Henry now had a son, Edsel. Edsel was only three days old and Clara, Henry's wife, was very ill. Henry wanted more money for his family. And he wanted to buy more things for his new engine too. Those were bad days in the life of Henry Ford.

Then, at the end of November, Henry got more money. The Edison Company was happy with his work. So he now got $75 a month. And then he got some help with his new engine too. An old friend, Fred Strauss, wanted to make a gasoline engine. So the two friends worked on it in the evenings.

In after years, Fred Strauss said, "I *worked* on the engine. Henry *talked* about it. Henry was a good talker."

At ten years old, with his first tin engine, Henry said to his young friends, "Do this! Do that!" Now he was a man, but he still talked to his friends in the same way.

After many months, the engine was ready. It was a good engine. Small, but good.

"What are you going to do with it?" Clara asked.

"I'm going to sell it to a friend. It can go on his boat."

Henry made two more boat engines after that. But he was still poor. And he still wanted more money.

The Quadricycle

Henry wanted to build a car. There were one or

two cars on the roads of Detroit now. They weren't very good cars. They had big, slow engines. Henry wanted to build a car with a small fast engine. So he worked on the car every night. In 1896, Henry still worked for the Edison Company. But he now worked for them in the daytime. At night, with his friend, Bishop, he worked in a building behind his house, at 58 Bagley Road, Detroit.

Then, one June night, it was ready.

"I'm going to take it on the road," he said.

"You can't do that!" said Clara. "It's three o'clock in the morning! All the people in the street are asleep!"

"It's ready now, so I'm going to drive it now!" said Ford.

He named his car 'The Quadricycle' – the four-wheeler – then jumped up onto it. "Run the engine!" he said to Bishop. The engine went round . . .

Then Ford stopped the engine and got down.

"I can't get it out of the building," he said. "I can't get it out of the door!"

Clara and Bishop looked at the door of the building. They looked at the big car. Yes. Henry was right.

"What are you going to do?" asked Bishop. Henry had the answer.

"The door must come down!" he said. "Stand back!" In half an hour, the front of the building

"He named his car 'The Quadricycle' — the four-wheeler."

was on the ground! But Henry wasn't sorry!

"*Now* I can get it through!" he said. "Run the engine again, Bishop!"

Ford jumped onto the Quadricycle and went out into the night. Bishop jumped onto his bicycle and went after him. They went up Grand Avenue, and wheeled right onto Washington Boulevard. Then, the car stopped in front of the Cadillac Hotel. All the people in the hotel looked out of their windows. But Ford and Bishop never saw them.

"What's wrong with it?" said Bishop.

"Nothing much," said Henry. They played with the engine for half an hour and after that it was ready.

At five o'clock in the morning, they came back to Ford's house.

"What are you going to do now?" asked Clara.

"I'm going to bed," said Henry.

The Years of Sleep

It was Henry's big day. Clara dressed Edsel, their son, in his Sunday clothes. Then they jumped up onto the Quadricycle.

"Dearborn, here we come!" said Henry.

All his life, Henry wanted to please his father. Now, with his new car, Henry was happy.

"After all these years, I can give my father something," he said to Clara. "After today, he can look at me and say, 'My son Henry is a big man!' "

At his father's farm, Henry jumped down. All the family were there; brothers and sisters and friends.

"Here we are!" said Henry. "What do you think of the Quadricycle? We came from Detroit in half an hour! What do you think about that?"

His father said nothing.

"Come for a drive," said Henry.

"No," said William Ford. "I don't want to get onto that thing. I'm happy with my horses!"

For a long time after that, Henry worked very little on his new car. There were now a lot of cars on the roads. But they weren't Ford cars. They came from the big, new car factories like Packards and Olds.

In 1898, Henry came home and said to Clara, "I'm going to sell my car. Mr C Ainsley's going to give me $200 for it."

Clara said nothing.

The years from 1896-1905 were dead years in the story of Henry Ford. He walked through them like a sleep-walker. Sometimes he jumped up and wanted to work again. He worked on a car, or an engine, for a short time. Perhaps a month. Then he went back to sleep again.

He changed his work many times. Rich people often wanted to help him. They put money into his cars. He was still, sometimes, a good talker. But he talked a lot and worked very little. So the money always went in the end.

Then, in 1905, William Ford, Henry's father, died. And Henry came back to life again.

The Fight Back

"You want a fight? OK, you can have one!" Henry looked at the sea of faces in front of him. Old John S Grey, Alexander Malcolmson, John Anderson, Horace Rackham, Vernon C Fry, Harold Wills. They were all rich men. And they were all wrong!

In 1905, cars were the playthings of the rich. No car-maker wanted to make a car for poor people.

"The poor don't have the money for cars!" said Malcolmson.

"Some of them can find $600," said Ford. "We can make cars for that."

"$600! You're wrong in the head, man!" said Malcolmson. "*I'm* not putting any money into a $600 car!"

Ford eyed the men around the table. "Think

about it. There are only a small number of rich people in this country. But there are a lot of poor people. We can sell more cars to them!"

"Perhaps you're right," said John Anderson.

"No, he's not!" said Malcolmson. "You can never sell a $600 car! Only rich people want cars. And they want them big and beautiful. I'm not giving Ford any money for a $600 car! I don't want to end my days a poor man!"

By 1910, Malcolmson had no money. And Henry Ford was a millionaire.

The Runabout

In 1906, the new Ford Motor Company made their $600 car. People all over America wanted to buy one. They named it 'The Runabout'. It was small and fast. It went at 72 kilometres an hour. In 1906 that *was* fast!

In that first year, Ford made 8000 cars. He wanted to make more, but his factory buildings were still small.

"I must buy more land for a big factory," he said to Clara. "Then, every farmer in America can buy a Ford car. With a car, a farmer can take his wood, or his animals, or his vegetables to the town every day. Young people can come into town in the evenings and have a good time. Country

"The Runabout, 1906."

women can go and see their friends for tea and talk. Yes. With cars, life can be good for country people. Without cars, every day is the same – long hours of dirty work with sleep at the end of it."

"But how can you buy more land?" said Clara. "You don't have the money."

"I'm not going to ask for money at the bank," said Henry. "I think, for a time, I must ask more money for a Runabout. Then, with the money, I can build a new factory. After that, I can build more cars so the cost of the Runabout can come down again. Perhaps we can get it down to only $500!"

The Model T Ford

In 1907, Ford had his new factory but he still wasn't happy. He wanted to work on a new car. "The Runabout's OK," he said, "but I want something more . . . "

The new car must have a very good engine. It must be small and fast. It must drive well on bad country roads. It must be a good car for women and for men. And, it must cost very little. It must be the car for the People of America.

He worked on the car for a year, and then it was ready. October 1st, 1908, was the big day. On that day, the Model T Ford went out onto the roads of America.

The Model T wasn't a beautiful car. She was small and black. But she had a very good engine with a long life. The people named her 'Tin Lizzie'. Ford made fifteen million of them in nineteen years.

The people loved her. They made songs and stories about her. She went along bad roads, through rivers and up mountains. Henry was very happy with his new car.

But he still wanted something more . . .

Edsel was now a young man and ready to work with his father. One day, Henry walked round his new factory with his son. The factory was very big and it had many buildings.

"Look at those men!" said Henry. "They're always walking around. They walk around for half the day! They do a little work on one car here. Then they go and get some new parts from that building over there. Then they come back and put the new parts in the car."

"But all factories are like that!" said Edsel.

"I'm going to change things around here," said Henry. "The men must stop in one place all day. They come here for work, not for a walk! The new parts and the men must be in the same building. Then the men have more time for work. And I can build more cars!"

In 1911, Henry made 34 000 cars. But he still

"Tin Lizzie, 1908."

". . . every man makes only a small part of a car."

wanted to make more. He said to Edsel, "Those men are still walking around a lot!"

"Yes," said Edsel. "Every man makes two or three parts for every car. They make one thing and then, perhaps, they must go across the building and make something more. After that, they walk back again."

"It's no good," said Henry. "Time is money. I'm going to change things again. From now, every man makes only one small part of a car."

In 1912, Henry made 78 440 cars. But he still wasn't happy.

After a time, he said to Edsel again. "Those men are *still* walking! They must stop in one place! The parts can go to the men!"

"How?" asked Edsel.

"The men can stand in a line," Henry said. "And a line of car-parts can run by in front of them. The first man does a little work on the first part. Then the part goes along the line to Man Number Two. *He* does a little work on it. Then it goes to Man Number Three. And so, at the very end of the line, you have a new car!"

In 1913, the Ford Motor Company made 168 304 cars. 60 cars every hour. There were a lot of Ford factories all over the world now. But Henry Ford still wanted more . . .

"Some of these lines of car-parts are very near the ground," he said. "And some of them are a long way up in the air. It's bad for the men's

"Henry and Edsel with one of their tractors."

backs." He changed the lines. Sometimes he changed the workers around too. He put the small men on the lines near the ground. And he put tall men on tall lines.

That wasn't all. "I'm going to give every man $5 a day," he said. "I want good, happy workers. Good, happy workers make more cars. And they can work only eight hours a day, not nine."

In 1914, Ford made 248 307 cars. There were now half a million Tin Lizzies in America. And every Tin Lizzie was $440.

But Henry Ford still wasn't happy.

The Farm Engine

In 1876, the thirteen-year-old Henry said to his father and brothers, "One day, I'm going to build engines for farm-work. Engines are going to do the work of men and horses." Now, in 1916, it was true.

With some of the money from Tin Lizzie, Henry made tractors. And where was his tractor factory? It was at Dearborn, on his father's old farm!

And then, Henry was happy!

A Word Game

This word game tells you something about Henry Ford. Answer the twenty questions, and write the answers in the boxes. Then read down the words in the grey boxes.

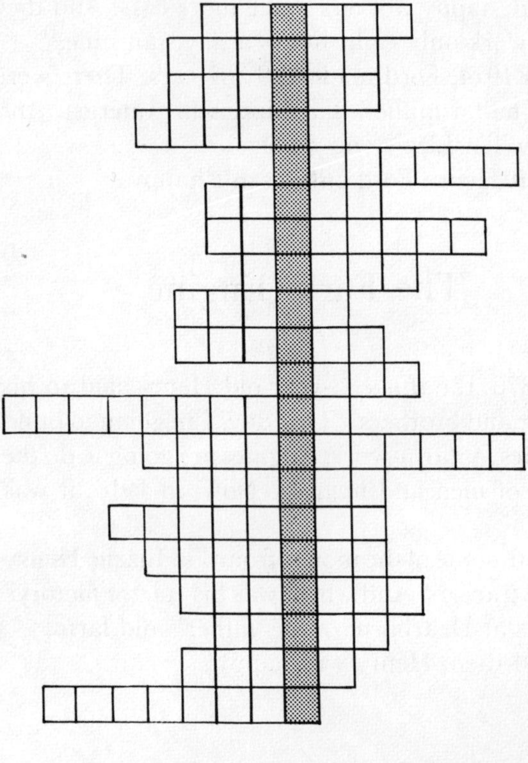

1 Henry made his first tin engine near this building.
2 "Look! The ____ are going round now!"
3 This man works on his land. William Ford was one.
4 A horse or a cat?
5 The Ford family lived 15 kilometres from this place.
6 "____-engines are no good on the land."
7 They had trains, and now they had ____.
8 This man made the first gasoline engine in America.
9 Henry Ford's wife.
10 Ford worked for this company.
11 Not slow.
12 They went up Grand Avenue and wheeled right onto ____ Boulevard.
13 The name of Ford's first four-wheeler.
14 Rich ____ often wanted to help him.
15 The name of Ford's first $600 car.
16 "I must buy more land for a big ____."
17 Ford lived in this country.
18 Mr and Mrs; man and ____.
19 The name of Ford's son.
20 Where was Ford's first tractor factory in America?

Answers:

1 school 2 wheels 3 farmer 4 animal 5 Detroit 6 steam 7 bicycles 8 Maxim 9 Clara 10 Edison 11 fast 12 Washington 13 Quadricycle 14 people 15 Runabout 16 factory 17 America 18 woman 19 Edsel 20 Dearborn